MW00593473

WG

The Book of
Christmas Wisdom

The Book of
Christmas Wisdom

By Criswell Freeman

WALNUT GROVE PRESS
Nashville, TN 37211

ISBN 1-58334-040-8

The ideas expressed in this book are not, in all cases, exact quotations, as some have been edited for clarity and brevity. In all cases, the author has attempted to maintain the speaker's original intent. In some cases, material for this book was obtained from secondary sources, primarily print media. While every effort was made to ensure the accuracy of these sources, the accuracy cannot be guaranteed. For additions, deletions, corrections or clarifications in future editions of this text, please write WALNUT GROVE PRESS.

Unless otherwise noted, Bible verses are taken from the King James Version

Scripture taken from the HOLY BIBLE INTERNATIONAL VERSION® Copyright ©1973, 1978, 1984, by International Bible Society. Used by permission of Zondervan Publishing House. All Rights Reserved.

Scripture taken from the NEW AMERICAN STANDARD BIBLE®, Copyright © 1960, 1962, 1963, 1971, 1972, 1973, 1975, 1977, 1995 by The Lockman Foundation. Used by permission.

Printed in the United States of America
Typesetting by Sue Gerdes
Cover Design by Bart Dawson
1 2 3 4 5 6 7 8 9 10 • 99 00 01 02 03 04 05

ACKNOWLEDGMENTS
The author gratefully acknowledges the helpful support of Dick and Mary Freeman, Angela Freeman, Sue Gerdes, Jim Gallery, Margaret Queen, and the entire staff of Walnut Grove Press.

For All Those Who Seek to Share

The True Meaning of Christmas

Table of Contents

Introduction

Perhaps Christmas is over, and you're now taking a few quiet moments to reflect on the holidays. Or perhaps you're still waiting for Santa to make his grand entrance. In either case, I hope the words on these pages will add a sense of comfort and perspective to your holiday season.

This book contains a Santa-sized portion of Christmas wisdom from an assortment of clergymen, writers, entertainers, and humorists. These pages remind us that Christmas is, above all, the season when we celebrate Christ's birth. That celebration is meant to be a time of generosity, hope, good will, and thanksgiving.

May this be a memorable and joyous holiday season for you and yours. And may the words on these pages find their way into your heart on Christmas Day *and* every other day of the year.

Criswell Freeman

1

The Christmas Story

The Christmas Story begins in a faraway land: a babe is born, and the world is forever changed.

The timeless words that follow are taken from The Gospel According to Saint Luke. These passages convey the wonder and majesty of Christ's birth...

And it came to pass in those days, that there went out a decree from Caesar Augustus, that all the world should be taxed.

And all went to be taxed, every one into his own city. And Joseph also went up from Galilee, out of the city of Nazareth, into Judea, unto the city of David, which is called Bethlehem; (because he was of the house and lineage of David) to be taxed with Mary his espoused wife, being great with child.

And so it was, that, while they were there, the days were accomplished that she should be delivered. And she brought forth her firstborn son, and wrapped him in swaddling clothes, and laid him in a manger; because there was no room for them in the inn.

And there were in the same country shepherds abiding in the field, keeping watch over their flock by night. And, lo, the angel of the Lord came upon them, and the glory of the Lord shone round about them: and they were sore afraid.

And the angel said unto them, Fear not: for, behold, I bring you good tidings of great joy, which shall be to all people. For unto you is born this day in the city of David a Savior which is Christ the Lord.

And this shall be a sign unto you; Ye shall find the babe wrapped in swaddling clothes, lying in a manger. And suddenly there was with the angel a multitude of the heavenly host praising God and saying, Glory to God in the highest, and on earth peace, good will toward men.

And it came to pass, as the angels were gone away from them into heaven, the shepherds said one to another, Let us now go even unto Bethlehem, and see this thing which is come to pass, which the Lord hath made known unto us. And they came with haste, and found Mary, and Joseph, and the babe lying in a manger.

And when they had seen it, they made known abroad the saying which was told concerning this child. And all they that heard it wondered at those things which were told them by the shepherds. But Mary kept all these things, and pondered them in her heart. And the shepherds returned, glorifying and praising God for all the things that they had heard and seen, as it was told unto them.

From the Second Chapter of
The Gospel According to Saint Luke,
King James Version

2

The Reason for the Season

No amount of commercialism or fanfare should obscure the fact that Christmas time is the annual birthday party of the Christian faith. Christmas day is, first and forever, a religious holiday — a time for Christians everywhere to rejoice, to pray, and to give heartfelt thanks.

Noted theologian Karl Barth observed, "Today, the Christmas message is delivered — the message of the light of the world which breaks through from above, always from above...."

During this time of Christmas, it is proper that we keep our eyes and our hearts lifted upwards, always upwards, as we joyfully celebrate the reason for the Christmas season: Christ Jesus.

Silent Night

Silent Night! Holy Night!
All is calm, all is bright.
Round yon virgin mother and child!
Holy infant so tender and mild,
Sleep in heavenly peace,
Sleep in heavenly peace.

Silent Night! Holy Night!
Shepherds quake at the sight!
Glories stream from heaven afar,
Heavenly hosts sing Alleluia!
Christ the Savior is born!
Christ the Savior is born!

Silent Night! Holy Night!
Son of God, love's pure light;
Radiant beams from Thy holy face,
With the dawn of redeeming grace,
Jesus Lord, at Thy birth,
Jesus Lord, at Thy birth.

by Father Joseph Mohr, 1818

The light of the world is reborn in His glory
at the same season every year.
Let us bless each other and be joyful.

Katherine Anne Porter

Let us pray that we shall be able to welcome
Jesus at Christmas — not in the cold manger
of our heart, but in a heart full of love
and humanity.

Mother Teresa

The one message of Christmas
is the Christmas story. If it is false,
we are doomed. If it is true, as it must be,
it makes everything else in the world all right.

Harry Reasoner

The old message: "For unto you is born
this day in the city of David a Savior which is
Christ the Lord" is still the heart of Christmas.

Peter Marshall

A Christmas gift symbolizes the love
that Christians bear to one another,
in the name of the One who loved them all.

Donald Culross Peattie

This is Christmas: not the tinsel,
not the giving, not even the carols,
but the humble heart that receives anew
the wondrous gift, the Christ.

Frank McKibben

The whole meaning of Christmas can be
summed up in the miracle of Christ's birth.

Arthur Bryant

O holy Child of Bethlehem!
Descend to us, we pray;
Cast out our sin, and enter in,
Be born in us today.

Phillips Brooks

Wise men and shepherds followed the shine of a star which led them to a crib where they learned that God is love. We still believe it, and on Christmas day, we try to practice it.

Jessamyn West

The Nativity brings us within touching distance, so to speak, of our spiritual birth in God through grace.

Pope John Paul II

The Son of God became man to enable men to become sons of God.

C. S. Lewis

May the Christmas morning make us happy to be Thy children and the Christmas evening bring us to our beds with grateful thoughts, forgiving and forgiven — for Jesus' sake.

Henry Van Dyke

It is good to be children
sometimes, and never
better than at Christmas,
when its mighty Founder
was a child himself.

Charles Dickens

May this Christmas increase the birth and
presence of God in your souls.

Pope John Paul II

I believe that the eternal lesson of Christmas
is to inspire us to use our God-given gifts
to build a better world.

Norman Vincent Peale

Christmas means the beginning
of Christianity — and a second chance
for the world.

Peter Marshall

The magic message of Christmas is
that God gave us so much more than
we can possibly give back!

Norman Vincent Peale

At Christmas,
surroundings do not
matter because the spirit
of Jesus is everywhere,
knocking on the doors
of our hearts.

Norman Vincent Peale

3

Christmas Is...

Christmas is a magic time
    when anything can happen,
When reindeer fly and children try
    to see straight through gift wrappin'.

Christmas is a magic time for kids
    and dogs and toys,
And a big red guy with an elf nearby
    who enchants the girls and boys.

Christmas is a well-trimmed tree,
    with presents underneath.
It's mistletoe, and ribbon bows,
    and a home-made holly wreath.

Christmas is a family time
    and a time of true thanksgiving
For the gift of life and that holy night,
    and the privilege of living,

Through one more joyous Christmas day;
    it's a gift from God above,
Because Christmas time is that day sublime
    when we share Christ's gift...of love.

Criswell Freeman

Christmas, like God, is timeless and eternal.

Dale Evans

Christmas is a mood, a quality, a symbol.
It is never merely a fact.

Howard Thurman

Christmas is a necessity. There has to be
at least one day of the year to remind us
that we're here for something else
besides ourselves.

Eric Sevareid

Christmas is the day
that holds all time together.

Alexander Smith

Christmas is most truly
Christmas when we
celebrate it by giving
the light of love to those
who need it most.

Ruth Carter Stapleton

Christmas is not in the stores, but in the hearts of people.

Anonymous

Every time we love, every time we give, it's Christmas.

Dale Evans

Christmas is the glorious time
of great Too-Much.

Leigh Hunt

Christmas is sights, especially the sights
of Christmas reflected in the eyes of a child.

William Saroyan

Christmas is the season for kindling the fire
of hospitality in the hall, the genial flame
of charity in the heart.

Washington Irving

Christmas is doing a little something extra
for someone.

Charles Schulz

Christmas,
in its final essence,
is for grown people
who have forgotten
what children know.
Christmas is for whoever
is old enough to have
denied the unquenchable
spirit of man.

Margaret Cousins

Christmas is a big love affair to remove the
wrinkles of the year with kindly remembrances.
John Wanamaker

Christmas is to every child, in his own way,
the wonder of the world and the light of life.
William Saroyan

As long as we know in our hearts
what Christmas *ought* to be, Christmas *is*.
Eric Sevareid

Christmas is being together — gathering
together. It is the time of the heart's inventory.
It is the time of going home in many ways.
William Saroyan

Surely Christmas is the very best time
   of the year to be home with loved ones.

W. Herschel Ford

Christmas is the season of joy,
   of holiday greetings exchanged, of gift-giving,
         and of families united.

Norman Vincent Peale

Christmas is a together time.

Charles Schulz

Christmas is a day of meaning and traditions,
a special day spent in the warm circle of family
         and friends.

Margaret Thatcher

Christmas isn't just a day, it's a frame of mind.

Valentine Davies
From *Miracle on 34th Street*

4

The Spirit of Christmas

Norman Vincent Peale writes, "Christmas waves a magic wand over the world, and behold, everything is softer and more beautiful." Such is the power of Christmas: Once the spirit of the season enters our hearts, the world takes on a softer glow, whether we're sitting by the fire in snow-covered Vermont or lounging on the beach in sunny Key West.

Sometimes the Christmas spirit remains elusive during the big buildup before The Big Day. As we hurry to buy last-minute gifts and goodies, we may feel temporarily overwhelmed. But ready or not, Christmas arrives, as it always does, at the same time each year; if we're wise, we welcome it with as much serenity as we can muster.

When we plant the seeds of the Christmas spirit deep within our souls, we experience a magical transformation. We change the world by changing the way we see it: Everything glows. And the Christmas spirit lives on because it lives within us.

Christmas brings out the spirituality
we sense within.

Leo Buscaglia

The spirit of Christmas brightens
even the darkest life.

Pamela Bujarski

The true spirit of Christmas calls for gifts,
but for thoughtful gifts,
not necessarily expensive gifts.

Lionel Barrymore

I always believed that the true spirit of
Christmas demands thought and effort
on the giver's part, not just lavish spending.

Inez Hogan

May we not "spend" Christmas or "observe" Christmas, but rather "keep" it.

Peter Marshall

Remember, if Christmas isn't found in your heart, you won't find it under the tree.

Charlotte Carpenter

We should try to hold on to the Christmas spirit, not just one day a year, but all 365.

Mary Martin

If you can keep Christmas for a day, why not always?

Henry Van Dyke

The Christmas spirit that survives
until Easter — or after — is the essence
of Christianity.

Isabel Currier

The Christmas spirit — love —
changes hearts and lives.

Pat Boone

They err who think Santa Claus comes down
through the chimney; he really enters
through the heart.

Mrs. Paul M. Ell

The Spirit of Christmas is the Light
of the world.

Dorothy Walworth Crowell

Unless we make
Christmas an occasion
to share our blessings,
all the snow in Alaska
won't make it "white."

Bing Crosby

The joy of brightening other lives, bearing
each others' burdens, and filling empty hearts
is the real magic of Christmas.

W. C. Jones

It is the personal thoughtfulness, the warm
human awareness, the reaching out of the self
to one's fellow man that makes giving worthy of
the Christmas spirit.

Isabel Currier

The only real blind person at Christmastime
is he who has not Christmas in his heart.

Helen Keller

My idea of Christmas, whether old-fashioned
or modern, is very simple: loving others.
Come to think of it, why do we have to wait
for Christmas to do that?

Bob Hope

To celebrate the heart of Christmas is
to forget ourselves in the service of others.

Henry C. Link

Of course, this is the season to be jolly,
but it is also a good time to be thinking about
those who aren't.

Helen Valentine

We cannot give in the true Christmas spirit
if we do not give to those who cannot afford
to give anything in return.

Clare Booth Luce

The more you spend in blessing,
The poor and lonely and sad,
The more of your heart's possessing,
Returns to make you glad.

John Greenleaf Whittier

Christmas day is a day
of joy and charity.
May God make you
very rich in both.

Phillips Brooks

"Maybe Christmas,"
he thought, "Doesn't
come from a store.
Maybe Christmas…
perhaps…means
a little bit more."

Dr. Seuss

5

Christmas Cheer

Victor Hugo wrote, "Cheerfulness is like money well expended in charity; the more we dispense of it, the more we possess." And so it goes at Christmas time. The more we share of Christmas cheer, the more we have left over for ourselves.

So why not vow this year to spread more cheerfulness than ever? Here's how: Put a smile on your face and a good word on the tip of your tongue. Turn on the Christmas music and hum a favorite song all day long. Pour a glass of eggnog and offer it to a friend. Speak kindly to every clerk, cashier, neighbor, family member, and coworker. Then, as you brighten your own little world, you'll make our great big world a happier, gentler, merrier place. And that's good because this old world needs all the holiday cheer it can get — and so do you.

At Christmas, play and
make good cheer,
For Christmas comes
but once a year.

Thomas Tusser

A Christmas family-party!
We know of nothing in nature more delightful!
Charles Dickens

Christmas is coming. Unhappiness seems
to be driven from our minds at this season,
along with cynicism and negativism.
Norman Vincent Peale

Be happy. It is one way of being wise.
Colette

The cheerful heart has a continual feast.
Proverbs 15:15 NIV

Heap on more wood!
  The wind is chill, But let it whistle as it will,
    We'll keep our Christmas merry still.

Sir Walter Scott

When I'm looking at a well-decorated
  Christmas tree, no amount of adverse
  experience can convince me that people
    are anything but good.

Andy Rooney

This will be the best Christmas
    we have ever had. It has to be
      because it always is.

Ferrol Sams

Which Christmas is the most vivid to me?
  It's always the next Christmas.

Joanne Woodward

Music awakens my Christmas spirit.

Julie Andrews

Christmas songs help us feel young in spirit,
even though we may be older in years.

Norman Vincent Peale

Bells are music's laughter.

Thomas Hood

Christmas, with its emphasis on generosity
and goodwill, provides its enthusiasts with
broad opportunities for self-expression.

Phillip Snyder

You have to be a child to know how wonderful
is a store window filled with dolls and
sleds and other toys.

Betty Smith

Children love best the old and familiar
family rituals.

Clare Booth Luce

Unshared joy is an unlit candle.

Spanish Proverb

The life without festival is a long road
without an inn.

Democritus of Abdera

I've seen what a good laugh can do.
It can transform tears into hope.

Bob Hope

Against the assault of laughter,
nothing can stand.

Mark Twain

One can endure sorrow alone,
but it takes two to be glad.

Elbert Hubbard

A cheerful look makes a dish a feast.

French Proverb

Then let every heart keep Christmas within.
Christ's pity for sorrow, Christ's hatred for sin,
Christ's care for the weakest,
Christ's courage for right,
Everywhere, everywhere,
Christmas tonight!

Phillips Brooks

Christmas trees stacked for sale are one
of the happiest sights in the world.

Andy Rooney

When the day dawns which ends
in Christmas Eve, an expectant hush comes
over our house, and we feel a sense of mystery.

Dorothy Walworth Crowell

Even though Christmas can be a lot of work,
we all know the bustle is worth the bother.

Lady Bird Johnson

Gifts of time and love
are surely the basic
ingredients of a truly
merry Christmas.

Peg Bracken

Be of good cheer; I have overcome the world.

Jesus
(John: 16:33)

6

Peace

In 1868, the noted American clergyman Phillips Brooks penned *O Little Town of Bethlehem*. This timeless hymn continues to brighten the lives and touch the hearts of Christians everywhere. The following familiar words convey the sense of peace that can — and should — be a part of every Christmas:

> O little town of Bethlehem,
> How still we see thee lie!
> Above thy deep and dreamless sleep
> The silent stars go by.

Sometimes, the quiet stillness of Christmas can be interrupted by the hustle-and-bustle preparations for Santa's big day. If your holiday season becomes a little too harried, slow down, be still, and look skyward as the silent stars go by. You will be reminded that God still sits in His heaven, and Christmas still offers peace on earth, a peace that can — and should — begin with you.

I heard the bells
on Christmas Day,
Their old familiar
carols play,
And wild and sweet
Their words repeat
Of peace on earth,
good-will to men!

Henry Wadsworth Longfellow

Glory and peace. Glory to God and peace
to men of good will. These are the immediate
and sublime effects of Christmas.

Giovanni Battista Cardinal Montini

Peace is not a season. It is a way of life.

Abbey Press

Peace is always beautiful.

Walt Whitman

Peace on earth and mercy mild
are still possible. On Christmas Eve,
all things are possible.

Gregg Easterbrook

Christmas began in the heart of God.
It is complete only when it reaches
the heart of man.

Religious Telescope

When we are preparing for Christmas, let us
refrain from hostile thoughts and words.

Raniero Cantalamessa

In His will is our peace.

Dante

The mind set on the Spirit is life and peace.

Romans 8:6 (NASB)

M ankind is a great, an immense family….
This is proved by what we feel in our hearts
at Christmas.

Pope John XXIII

 T he Lord blesses his people with peace.

Psalm 29:11 (NIV)

 A s fits the holy Christmas birth,
Be this, good friends, our carol still —
Be peace on earth, be peace on earth,
To men of gentle will.

William Makepeace Thackery

 P eace is our final good.

St. Augustine

Angels come down,
    with Christmas in their hearts,
   Gentle, whimsical, laughing, heaven-sent,
   And, for a day, fair Peace have given me.

Vachel Lindsay

Peace, like every other rare and precious thing,
  doesn't come to you. You have to go and get it.

Faith Forsyte

What a blessing Christmas is!
    What it does for friendship.

D. D. Monroe

I truly believe that if we keep telling the
  Christmas story, singing the Christmas songs,
and living the Christmas spirit, we can bring joy
   and happiness and peace to this world.

Norman Vincent Peale

Christmas is, of course, the time
to be home — in heart as well as body.

Garry Moore

This is the message of Christmas:
We are never alone.

Taylor Caldwell

Santa Claus is everywhere —
but even the children might get more out of
Christmas if they knew more about Him
whose birthday it is.

William F. French

As the children grow older, peace settles
in on the house at Christmastime.

Lady Bird Johnson

On this Christmas,
may we, the people
of every race, nation, and
religion, learn to love one
another and to forgive
and be forgiven.
Then the peace
of Christ will prevail.

Coretta Scott King

What sweeter music can we bring
Than a carol for to sing
The birth of this our heavenly king.

Robert Herrick

We must banish doubt and fear, and we
must still believe in the Golden Rule for all
mankind. Then, it can be a happy Christmas.

Franklin D. Roosevelt

And so, at this Christmastime, I greet you.
Not quite as the world sends greetings, but
with the prayer that for you, now and forever,
the day breaks and shadows flee away.

Fra Giovanni

We must all continue, especially at this time
of year, to try and fulfill this grand dream:
Peace on earth.

Elizabeth Taylor

Peace I leave with you, my peace I give unto you.

Jesus
(John 14:27)

7

Christmas Memories

No season carries with it as many memories as the holiday season. As December 25th approaches, we are confronted with a double dose of memory-evoking events: the end of another year and the passing of another Christmas. No wonder we find ourselves reflecting on the past!

May Sarton writes, "A holiday gives one a chance to look backward and forward, to reset oneself by an inner compass." This year, as you reset your inner compass, give thanks for past and future blessings. Keep the memories of bygone holidays and departed loved ones warm in your heart. Remember that this Christmas and every Christmas you're making memories, and it's up to you, not Santa, to make them great.

The idea that Christmas is only for children is nonsense. The longer we live, the more Christmas means.

Dorothy Walworth Crowell

Christmas is the keeping-
place for memories
of our innocence.

Joan Mills

For children, Christmas
is anticipation. For adults,
Christmas is memory.

Eric Sevareid

Christmas is the most evocative and
nostalgic day of the year.

Clare Booth Luce

Christmas conjures up images we know
from memories too deeply a part of our
universal consciousness ever to fade.

Leo Buscaglia

You remember hundreds of Christmas
moments, and you laugh — or weep —
with the dearest of them.

Margaret Lee Runbeck

How many dormant sympathies
does Christmas awaken.

Charles Dickens

To me, an old-fashioned Christmas means old-fashioned values — like sharing Christmas Eve and Christmas Day with your loved ones.

Robert Wagner

My love of Christmas has not diminished, and I am grateful to have seen so many Christmases. But if I were asked which ones stick in the memory most vividly, I would have to say those earliest ones.

James Beard

Family traditions mean so very much to children.

Fred Rogers

My first copies of *Treasure Island* and *Huckleberry Finn* still have some blue-spruce needles scattered in the pages. They smell of Christmas still.

Charlton Heston

When we recall Christmas
past, we usually find that
the simplest things —
not the great occasions —
give off the greatest glow
of happiness.

Bob Hope

At Christmas, all roads lead home.

Marjorie Holmes

Something about an old-fashioned Christmas
is hard to forget.

Hugh Downs

Each year that we repeat a family tradition,
it becomes more special.

Lynne Laukhuf

We recall the special Christmases that are
like little landmarks in a life of a family.

Marjorie Holmes

There are always fleeting moments of sadness
at Christmas. If they're only fleeting,
you're lucky.

Andy Rooney

Christmas is a time when you get homesick — even when you're home.

Carol Nelson

As another Christmas passes, the memory of it stays and hovers like the scent of cedar. And even if it can't be Christmas all the year, memories remain.

Minnie Pearl

This is the hour, unique in the whole year, of Christmas Eve. It is always the same and always different.

Pearl Buck

Christmas was coming. Everywhere was a sense of rousedness. Everyone was preparing for something.

D. H. Lawrence

The song *White Christmas* still evokes my own Christmas memories. It does, I suppose, because it celebrates more than a holiday — it symbolizes home.

Ronald Reagan

The song *White Christmas*
is like an old Christmas
memory: It inspires
a happy sadness
in the heart.

Bing Crosby

There was a special excitement in the kitchens, as many of the things we prepared were foods we tasted only at Christmas.

Edna Lewis

On Christmas Eve, the whole house used to tingle with suppressed excitement. It still does.

Bing Crosby

Family gatherings have been the essence of my Christmas for as long as I can remember.

Henry Mancini

As you get older, you may think Christmas has changed. It hasn't. It's you who have changed.

Harry Truman

Μy Christmas wish is that for a little while
I might know and live again in the world I knew
when I was ten years old.

Paul Gallico

I suppose every adult has a secret dream
of reviving a childhood Christmas.

Charlton Heston

Shining from the twinkling trees of Christmas
— tall and tiny, splendid and simple — is each
family's own special viewpoint, a sentimental
mixture of traditions and cherished memories.

Margaret Davidson

Christmas should be remembered for the
scents of pine, oranges, ginger and cloves.

Eugene McCarthy

Christmas was a great day:
The presents were inexpensive and received
with much joy and gratification.

Will Rogers

As a kid, sometimes my Christmas present
was an orange. We were poor and fruit was a
once-a-year thing. To this day, that's why I still
love the smell of oranges.

Dolly Parton

When I was a kid, Christmas was always a
very painful day for me. I used to put my
stockings on without taking the walnuts out.

Bob Hope

In memory, everything seems to happen
to music.

Tennessee Williams

Memories of hymns and carols
keep the spirit of Christmas fresh.

Norman Vincent Peale

The best Christmas was the one when I was
five, before worldliness and wisdom
began to set in.

Charles Kuralt

Christmas went on and on as it always had
and always will, forever and ever and ever.

Pearl Buck

Christmas, my child, is always.

Dale Evans

<u>8</u>

Joy

John Greenleaf Whittier understood the true spirit of Christmas when he wrote,

> Somehow not only for Christmas
> But all the long year through,
> The joy that you give to others
> Is the joy that comes back to you.

At Christmas time, we get what we give. When we give of ourselves and give from the heart, Christmas becomes a time of celebration and joy.

So take a hint from Mr. Whittier: As the bells begin to jingle and Santa puts the finishing touches on his list, keep a smile on your face and a carol in your heart. Because on Christmas day, and all the other days as well, the happiness you share is ultimately the happiness that you are allowed to keep.

Christmas Eve is still the most exciting day
of the year.

Minnie Pearl

On Christmas Eve, the faces of people are
more alive than on any other day of the year.

Carl Sandburg

It is not even the beginning of Christmas
unless it is Christmas in the heart.

Richard Roberts

The more joy we have, the more nearly
perfect we are.

Spinoza

I think Christmas really works when you can see it through the enthusiastic, joyous eyes of children waiting for Santa Claus and all the goodies.

Robert Stack

It is Christmas
in the heart that puts
Christmas in the air.

W. T. Ellis

At Christmas, Dear Lord, give us the faith of innocent children. Let our hearts swell and let us live, if only for a day, with the hope and joy we knew as children.

Anonymous

Joy is not in things, it is in us.

Ben Franklin

If you have no joy in your religion, there's a leak in your Christianity somewhere.

Billy Sunday

Joy is the serious business of heaven.

C. S. Lewis

The joy of the Lord is your strength.

Nehemiah 8:10

Joy is the flag you fly when the Prince of Peace
is in residence within your heart.

Wilfred Peterson

Don't deprive yourself of the joy of giving.

Michael Greenberg

The gift of the Christ Child is that the saddest
and most difficult holidays may hold the seeds
and promise of future joy.

Mary Higgins Clark

It seems to me the secret of a joyful Christmas
— especially for children — lies in preserving
not only the holiday but also the Holy Day.

Clare Booth Luce

Grief can take care of itself, but to get
the full value of joy, you must have somebody
to share it with.

Mark Twain

Happiness is not perfected until it is shared.

Jane Porter

Those who bring sunshine into the lives
of others cannot keep it from themselves.

James M. Barrie

What brings joy to the heart is not so much
the friend's gift as the friend's love.

St. Ailred of Rievaulx

Give yourself at
Christmas; there really is
no more wonderful gift.

Dorothy Wilson

H appiness depends upon ourselves.

Aristotle

A merry heart doeth good like a medicine.

Proverbs 17:22

N o man truly has joy unless he lives in love.

St. Thomas Aquinas

M erry Christmas to you! May the glory
that we celebrate in this Christmas season
fill your life forever and ever.

Norman Vincent Peale

A child sees only delight and pleasure in the Christmas story. So maybe the Christmas message is just that — the possibility of recovering that childlike joy.

Harry Reasoner

Christmas — the best day of the year.

George Templeton Strong

The Christmas story gives its triumphant answer: "Be not afraid."

Karl Barth

Behold, I bring you good tidings of great joy, which shall be to all people.

Luke 2:10

9

Santa Claus

Little Virginia O'Hanlon believed in Santa Claus, but some of her friends had their doubts. So Virginia asked her father for a straight answer to the question, "Is there really a Santa Claus?" When Virginia's dad was evasive, the precocious young girl took it upon herself to write a letter to the Sun, a New York daily newspaper.

On September 21, 1897, Francis Church responded to Virginia's letter with an editorial that has become a Christmas classic. Virginia's letter and Mr. Church's response appear on the pages that follow, along with a few other observations about the Man in Red.

Today, as in Virginia's day, Santa's methods are cloaked in mystery. We can't see him come down the chimney, we don't understand how he makes his rounds, and we don't comprehend how he keeps up with such a big list — much less how he carries all those toys around in a single sleigh. But even if we can't understand Santa's ways, we do know that he is real. For proof, we need look no further than our own hearts. Because as long as Santa dwells in a single human heart — like yours — he lives.

Yes, Virginia,
There is a Santa Claus

Dear Editor,
I am eight years old.
Some of my little friends say
there is no Santa Claus.
Papa says, "If you see it in the Sun, it's so."
Please tell me the truth.

Virginia O'Hanlon

Virginia, your little friends are wrong. They have been affected by the skepticism of a skeptical age. They do not believe except they see. They think that nothing can be which is not comprehensible by their little minds. All minds, Virginia, whether they be men's or children's are little. In this great universe of ours, man is a mere insect, an ant in his intellect as compared with the boundless world about him, as measured by the intelligence capable of grasping the whole truth and knowledge.

Yes, Virginia, there is a Santa Claus. He exists as certainly as love and generosity and devotion exist, and you know how they abound and give to your life its highest beauty and joy. Alas! how dreary would be the world if there were no Santa Claus! It would be as dreary as if there were no Virginias. There would be no childlike faith then, no poetry, no romance to make tolerable this existence. We should have no enjoyment, except in sense and sight. The eternal light with which childhood fills the world would be extinguished.

Not believe in Santa Claus! You might as well not believe in fairies! You might get your papa to hire men to watch in all the chimneys on Christmas Eve to catch Santa Claus, but even if they did not see Santa Claus coming down, what would that prove? Nobody sees Santa Claus. The most real things in the world are those that neither children nor men can see.

No Santa Claus! Thank God he lives, and he lives forever. A thousand years from now, Virginia, nay ten times ten thousand years from now, he will continue to make glad the hearts of children.

The New York Sun, 1897

Christmas is sleeping
with one eye shut while
the other eye watches
for Santa Claus.

Charles Schulz

There's nothing so beautiful as a child's dream of Santa Claus.

Jay Frankston

Santa Claus is the fairy tale that comes alive
when we are old enough to understand the magic
of our parents' love.

Ina Hughes

Now the existence, the very spirit of Christmas
is this: that we first make believe a thing is so
and lo! it presently turns out to be so.

Stephen Butler Leacock

Santa's message is simply this:
Magical possibilities exist in the universe.

Sam Rosenberg

The fantasy of Santa Claus serves our children
well, in so many ways, that we as parents should
join them in wishing him season's greetings.

Bruno Bettelheim

Christmas is for children, but over the
years I've discovered that it's
the old fellow in the red suit who has
the very best time of all.

John P. Hayes

My Uncle Bill always dressed up like a fat
old man with whiskers playing Santa Claus.
Nobody was fooled, but we pretended
to be — that was part of the fun.

Katherine Anne Porter

There is something very real about Santa: He
personifies giving and the spirit of the holiday.

Fred Rogers

Yearly, newly, faithfully, truly, somehow
Santa Claus ALWAYS COMES!

Phyllis McGinley

The great thing is not to believe in Santa Claus; it is to be Santa Claus.

Pat Boone

10

Christmas Gifts

Christmas is the season for giving, but gift-giving need not be synonymous with commercialism. The holiday season is the perfect time to share spiritual gifts as well as material ones. Spiritual gifts, of course, endure and should take priority. But material gifts are also the order of the day, and that's why matters often become complicated as December 25th approaches.

As The Big Day nears, your shopping list may seem more weighty than the phone book. Don't panic! Simply remember that the very best gifts are not necessarily those with the highest price tags. The best gifts come directly from the heart, wrapped in love.

So the next time you find yourself shopping for that very special someone or someones, remember that timeless gifts always contain a portion of the giver. And while you're deciding on ways to make your holiday gifts instant keepsakes, consider the quotations that follow.

Giving is the secret of a healthy life,
giving not necessarily money, but whatever
one has of encouragement and sympathy
and understanding.

John D. Rockefeller, Jr.

A hand-made gift says, "I love you; you are
important to me; you are worthy of my time
and my best effort."

Catherine Marshall

Simple gifts such as a compliment, a note,
a telephone call or a simple act of kindness —
these are the truest forms of giving because
they come from the heart — they are literally
a portion of the giver.

David Dunn

Material gifts are always secondary
to spiritual gifts.

Rose Kennedy

For the rest of the year, we are usually preoccupied with getting. Christmas is a time which is marked by the glory of giving.

Roy Pearson

We make a living by what we get, but we make a life by what we give.

Winston Churchill

Charity gives itself rich; greed hoards itself poor.

German Proverb

Selfishness makes Christmas a burden; love makes it a delight.

Anonymous

He who gives to me teaches me to give.

Danish Proverb

There are all kinds of presents one can get
for Christmas. The best is love.

Helen Hayes

The only gift is a portion of thyself.

Ralph Waldo Emerson

My mother knew the real reason for any gift
was to make you feel special about yourself.

Nancy Eberle

I think the most precious
Christmas gift parents
can give their children
is time.

Fred Rogers

No matter what presents little children give, adults will find them endearing.

Carol Higgins Clark

God loves a cheerful giver.

II Corinthians 9:7 (NASB)

Christmas is light and laughter, love and tenderness, sympathy and good impulses. Giving! It is pure gold, and while love lasts, must endure.

A. M. Hopkins

It's the spirit in which the gift is rich.

Edmund Vance Cook

And every gift, though it be small,
is in reality great if given with affection.

Pindar

Don't assume that spending twice as much
will be twice as satisfying.

Amy Dacyczyn

When I was a boy, we didn't have much and
we didn't give much, but what we did have
seemed marvelous.

Bing Crosby

When we exchange gifts, we always stay
within our means. You see we once had
the good fortune of being poor.

Danny Thomas

The most splendid Christmas gift,
the most marveled and magic, is the gift
that has not yet been opened.

Gregg Easterbrook

Our children await Christmas presents
like politicians getting election results.

Marceline Cox

It may sound like a platitude and it may take
a long time to learn, but gifts of the heart
are the gifts that really matter.

Fred Rogers

Every charitable act is a steppingstone
toward heaven.

Henry Ward Beecher

Charity begins at home
but should not end there.

Scottish Proverb

We don't give outrageously expensive gifts. Christmas isn't a matter of showing off. You should give of yourself, not just your money.

Andy Williams

Christmas is the day when any gift, however small, should be gratefully received provided it is given with love.

Clare Booth Luce

Bounty always receives part of its value from the manner in which it is bestowed.

Samuel Johnson

No act of kindness is ever wasted, no matter how small.

Aesop

It is always pleasant to be generous.

Ralph Waldo Emerson

Being able to share with others
gives Christmas its meaning.

Michael Landon

The excellence of a gift lies in its
appropriateness rather than its value.

Charles Dudley Warner

We must not only give what we have, we must
also give what we are.

Désiré Joseph Mercier

What I want most at Christmas is simply this:
the gift of love.

Nancy Reagan

Oh, give your gifts
with spirit warm,
And not because
you must conform.

Kay Riley

L avishness is not generosity.

Thomas Fuller

G et not your friends by bare compliments,
but by giving them sensible tokens of love.

Socrates

G iving requires good sense.

Ovid

A gift in season is a double favor to the needy.

Publilius Syrus

I t is the intention, not the face-value of the gift,
that matters.

Seneca

This is the essence of the Christmas story:
a spirit of giving; giving not from a sense of duty,
not as a return for receiving, but from an
awareness that in a world where so much
is given to man, man too should
himself give gifts.

Anne Bryan McCall

A man there was, and they called him mad;
The more he gave, the more he had.

John Bunyon

It is more blessed to give than to receive.

Jesus (Acts 20:35, NASB)

In this world it is not what we take up,
but what we give up that matters.

Henry Ward Beecher

The closer it gets to Christmas, the quicker
I make decisions about presents.

Andy Rooney

Christmas is the season when people run out
of money before they run out of friends.

Larry Wilde

The race to get a Christmas present for Father
usually ends in a tie.

Gene Shalit

If any of you are still shopping for my Christmas
present, please get me one that is finished.
I've decided that my favorite word in the
English language is "pre-assembled."

Erma Bombeck

11

Decorations

In the 1820's the Christmas tree was introduced to England by German immigrants. By 1850 trees were more commonplace, and Charles Dickens wrote, "I have been looking on, this evening, at a merry company of children assembled round that pretty German toy, a Christmas tree." Today, of course, the Christmas tree is no longer a German oddity; it's a wintertime fixture and a symbol of the holiday season.

In this chapter, we consider the joys of a well-trimmed tree and the delights of a well-decorated hearth. These decorations lift our spirits by setting the proper mood for the holidays. Once the tree is trimmed (whether it's a king-sized fir or a tabletop model), the homeplace is ready for Santa's big night.

The hunt for the Christmas tree:
what a joyous day!

Mary Lindsay Hoffman

One of the nicest things about a Christmas
tree is that it looks good no matter
how you decorate it.

Phillip Snyder

The perfect Christmas tree?
All Christmas trees are perfect!

Charles N. Barnard

I am old-fashioned about Christmas. I love
the trees and decorations and lights and
tinsel. But most of all, I love the feeling of being
involved in something exciting and wonderful:
Christmas.

Joan Crawford

Christmas is a box of tree ornaments that have become part of the family.

Charles Schulz

And up at the tree was fixed a large star of
gold tinsel; it was magnificent beyond words.

Hans Christian Anderson

Christmas has, so far, withstood the threat
of artificial trees and plastic ornaments.

Eugene McCarthy

A green tree with its multicolored decorations
saved from year to year and lovingly added to,
is more beautiful than any artfully prepared
at the florist.

Virginia Scott Miner

The best Christmas trees
come very close
to exceeding nature.

Andy Rooney

Christmas must always be the celebration
of the Nativity of Lord Jesus. But it is also the
time of year of joy and color — the wrappings,
the decorations, the greens, and the reds.

Danny Thomas

For one night of the year, that otherwise
ordinary article of clothing is miraculously
transformed into a captivating catchall:
the stocking.

Meryle Evans

The orange has its place you know,
To fill each Christmas stocking toe.

Roseanne Russell

Bring forth the fir tree,
      The box and the bay.
      Deck out our cottage
      For glad Christmas day.
Old English Rhyme

So now is come our joyful feast,
      Let every man be jolly,
      Each room with ivy leaves is dressed
      And every post with holly.
George Wither

Have you seen God's Christmas tree in the sky
With its trillions of tapers blazing high?
Angela Morgan

Each of us creates our own special times at Christmas. We find our special ornaments, hang the mistletoe, and place the star as we have done before. There is a comforting certainty in the sameness — a promise of continuity.

Lady Bird Johnson

12

A Sampling of Christmas Verse

Every year Christmas changes, but every year some things remain the same: We sing the same carols, recite the same poems, watch the same movies, and listen to the same music. When it comes to Yuletide fare, our tastes are slow to change. Here we celebrate a few of the most enduring Christmas verses ever penned. May they live, unchanged, forever!

A Visit from St. Nicholas

'T was the night before Christmas,
    when all through the house
Not a creature was stirring, not even a mouse;
The stockings were hung by the chimney
    with care,
In hopes that St. Nicholas soon would be there.
The children were nestled all snug in their beds,
While visions of sugar-plums danced in
    their heads;
And mamma in her kerchief, and I in my cap,
Had just settled our brains for a long winter's
    nap;
When out on the lawn there arose such a clatter,
I sprang from my bed to see what was the matter.
Away to the window I flew like a flash,
Tore open the shutters and threw up the sash.
The moon on the breast of the new-fallen snow
Gave the luster of midday to objects below,
When, what to my wondering eyes should appear,
But a miniature sleigh and eight tiny reindeer,
With a little old driver, so lively and quick,
I knew in a moment it must be St. Nick.

More rapid than eagles his coursers they came,
And he whistled, and shouted, and called them
    by name:
"Now, Dasher! now, Dancer! now, Prancer
    and Vixen!
On, Comet! on, Cupid! on, Donner and Blitzen!
To the top of the porch, to the top of the wall!
Now dash away! dash away! dash away all!"
As dry leaves that before the wild hurricane fly,
When they meet with an obstacle, mount to the sky,
So up to the house-top the coursers they flew,
With the sleighful of toys, and St. Nicholas, too.
And then, in a twinkling, I heard on the roof
The prancing and pawing of each little hoof.
As I drew in my head, and was turning around,
Down the chimney St. Nicholas came with a bound.
He was dressed all in fur, from his head to his foot,
And his clothes were all tarnished
    with ashes and soot;
A bundle of toys he had flung on his back,
And he looked like a peddlar just opening his pack.
His eyes — how they twinkled! his dimples,
    how merry!
His cheeks were like roses, his nose like a cherry!
His droll little mouth was drawn up like a bow,
And the beard on his chin was as white as the snow.

The stump of a pipe he held tight in his teeth,
And the smoke it encircled his head
    like a wreath.
He had a broad face and a little round belly
That shook, when he laughed, like a bowl full
    of jelly.
He was chubby and plump, a right jolly old elf,
And I laughed, when I saw him, in spite of myself.
A wink of his eye and a twist of his head
Soon gave me to know I had nothing to dread.
He spoke not a word, but went straight
    to his work,
And filled all the stockings; then turned
    with a jerk,
And laying his finger aside of his nose,
And giving a nod, up the chimney he rose.
He sprang to his sleigh, to his team
    gave a whistle,
And away they all flew like the down of a thistle,
But I heard him exclaim, ere he drove
    out of sight,
"Happy Christmas to all, and to all a good-night!"

Clement C. Moore
1823

Jingle Bells

Dashing thro' the snow
in a one-horse open sleigh,
O'er the fields we go, laughing all the way;
Bells on bob-tail ring, making spirits bright;
What fun it is to ride and sing
a sleighing song tonight!

Jingle bells! Jingle bells! Jingle all the way!
Oh! what fun it is to ride
    in a one-horse open sleigh!

A day or two ago I thought I'd take a ride,
And soon Miss Fanny Bright
was seated by my side;
The horse was lean and lank,
misfortune seemed his lot,
He got into a drifted bank, and we,
we got upshot.

Jingle bells! Jingle bells! Jingle all the way!
Oh! what fun it is to ride
    in a one-horse open sleigh!

John Pierpoint
1827

Adeste Fideles

O come all ye faithful, joyful and triumphant,
O come ye, O come ye to Bethlehem.
Come and behold him, born the King of angels,

O come let us adore him,
O come let us adore him,
O come let us adore him,
Christ the Lord.

Sing, choirs of angels, sing in exultation,
Sing all ye citizens of heaven above,
Glory to God, all glory in the highest,

O come let us adore him,
O come let us adore him,
O come let us adore him,
Christ the Lord.

Latin Carol, 18ᵗʰ Century

O Little Town of Bethlehem

O little town of Bethlehem,
How still we see thee lie,
Above thy deep and dreamless sleep,
The silent stars go by;

Yet in thy dark streets shineth,
The everlasting Light,
The hopes and fears of all the years,
Are met in thee tonight.

O holy Child of Bethlehem!
Descend to us we pray;
Cast out our sin and enter in,
Be born in us today.

We hear the Christmas angels
The great glad tidings tell;
O come to us abide with us,
Our Lord Emmanuel!

Phillips Brooks, 1867

Away in a Manger

Away in a manger, no crib for a bed,
The little Lord Jesus lay down his sweet head.
The stars in the sky looked down where he lay,
The little Lord Jesus, asleep on the hay.

The cattle are lowing, the baby awakes,
But little Lord Jesus, no crying he makes.
I love Thee, Lord Jesus! Look down from the sky,
And stand by my cradle till morning is nigh.

Martin Luther

God Rest You Merry Gentlemen

God rest you merry, gentlemen,
Let nothing you dismay,
Remember Christ our Savior
Was born on Christmas day,
To save us all from Satan's pow'r
When we were gone astray;
O tidings of comfort and joy, comfort and joy,
O tidings of comfort and joy.

From God our heavenly Father,
A blessed angel came.
And unto certain shepherds,
Brought tidings of the same;
How that in Bethlehem was born
The Son of God by name;
O tidings of comfort and joy, comfort and joy,
O tidings of comfort and joy.

18th Century English Carol

It Came Upon a Midnight Clear

It came upon the midnight clear,
    that glorious song of old,
From angels bending near the earth,
    to touch their harps of gold.
Peace on the earth, goodwill to men,
    from heav'n's all gracious king,
The world in solemn stillness lay
    to hear the angels sing.

Edmund Sears, 1850

13

Christmas Advice

The following words of wisdom are intended as an antidote to the forces that might otherwise dim the lights of Christmas in your soul. Those forces, composed of a series of obligations to family, friends, and coworkers, can leave you feeling over-committed and under-appreciated. If so, this advice will help.

Christmas should be a time of joy, a time of contemplation and renewal. But Christmas, like every other event in your life, is what you make it. So make this holiday season the best ever by working from the inside-out. Start with a firm commitment to keep the true meaning of Christmas firmly planted in your heart. Then, once the "inner you" is focused on the spirit of the season, look upon the holidays not as a series of obligations, but as an opportunity for sharing. Share as much as you can with those you love and those in need, knowing that with a song in your heart and a word of thanksgiving on your lips, you and Santa will make a great team.

Let's not permit
the crowds and the rush
to crowd Christmas
out of our hearts…for
that's where it belongs.

Peter Marshall

Remember that having fun
is just as important an aspect of the holidays
as getting the presents wrapped.

Sonya Friedman

Forget, forgive; for who may say
that Christmas Day may ever come
to host or guest again.

William H. H. Murray

Above all, the family who wants a truly
happy Christmas will sing carols together.

Clare Booth Luce

Make a joyful noise unto the Lord.

Psalm 100:1

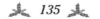

My philosophy? Eat the icing! Light those expensive candles! Use those pretty little soaps! Wear, use, and enjoy! There's no time more important than NOW! Happy holidays.

Erma Bombeck

The best way to avoid fatigue, panic, or depression is to try to keep in mind that Christmas is intended as a celebration, not a contest.

Sandra Boynton

Christmas needs a little less rushing about and a little more quiet thinking.

Helen Valentine

Christmas is a good time to take stock of our blessings.

Pat Boone

Never worry about the size of your
Christmas tree. In the eyes of children,
they are all 30 feet tall.

Larry Wilde

The most precious gift you can give your
children at Christmas is one that will stand
by them for all times, in all places and all
conditions: the gift of positive thinking.

Norman Vincent Peale

Here's my advice: Make a big thing
of Christmas, even if you're tired.

Harry Reasoner

Christmas, my child, is love in action.

Dale Evans

I read Dickens' *Christmas Carol* to my family.
What better reminder is there
of the real meaning of Christmas day?

Eleanor Roosevelt

Even the simplest of gifts can be made
attractive — and special —
by unique wrapping.

Katharine Fisher

If shopping makes you crazy, start earlier...
or give money.

Mary Hance

When it comes to your Christmas list,
focus on finishing. Try to get one thing done
before you start the next.

Jill Kirchner

Women are never what they seem to be.
There is the woman you see, and there is
the woman who is hidden. Buy the gift
for the woman who is hidden.

Erma Bombeck

Don't center your holiday on gift-giving.

Amy Dacyczyn

Don't buy anyone socks for Christmas.

Andy Rooney

Why not give a Bible for Christmas?

Good Housekeeping
December, 1959

Take this pledge:
"I solemnly swear to obey
the laws of low-volume
eating throughout the
entire holiday season."

Richard Simmons

Let the kids wrap gifts for the relatives.

Jill Kirchner

Have the kids write thank-you notes. They'll resist, but make sure they write them anyway.

Carole Owens

Thank-you letters should be sent long before it's time for Lent.

Kay Riley

It's Christmastime, so why not dare to dream the impossible dream?

Whitney Young, Jr.

One of the most glorious messes in the world is the mess created in the living room on Christmas day. Don't clean it up too quickly.

Andy Rooney

14

Observations About Christmas

We conclude with a few thoughts on The Best Day Of The Year. Merry Christmas.

Even though we try to keep the Christ in Christmas, very often we are overwhelmed with Santa's tinsel and Aunt Sophie's scarf.

Dom DeLuise

It seems to me that running around shopping malls, buying Christmas presents doesn't make you a Christian any more than going to a garage makes you a car.

Mickey Rooney

The Christmas season has come to mean the period when the public plays Santa Claus to the merchants.

John Haynes Holmes

Dashing through the dough....

Ralph M. Wyser

And on Christmas morning, after the gifts have been opened, what are the kids doing? Playing with boxes and snapping the air pockets of plastic packing material.

Erma Bombeck

I don't set myself up as a holy man, but I do
feel deeply about Christmas for what it is,
so I do everything I can to keep
Christmas traditional.

Perry Como

Christmas trees should be real except
where prohibited by fire codes.

Andy Rooney

Home for Christmas!
That's where everybody instinctively
wants to be for the great holiday.

Jerome Weidman

My fantasy for a perfect Christmas is set
long ago in New England and includes
a big family, church, dinner, and presents
followed by singing and sledding.

Gregory Peck

For Christmas weather, tradition calls for snow.
It seems almost impossible to imagine
an old-time Christmas without the mercury
somewhere near zero.

Phillip Snyder

I'm dreaming of a white Christmas,
Just like the ones I used to know.

Irving Berlin

You don't hear many holiday songs until
after Thanksgiving, but I get requests for
White Christmas all year round.

Bing Crosby

I wrote *The Christmas Song* with Bob Wells
in July of 1945...on the hottest day of the year.

Mel Tormé

The things we do at Christmas are touched
with a certain grain of extravagance,
as beautiful in some ways
as the extravagance of nature
in June.

Robert Collyer

Holidays are a time of profound, conflicting
emotions, close interaction with family and
friends, increased activity and special demands.

Carole Owens

There are always a few presents that resist
being wrapped at all. It is impossible
to wrap a bicycle.

Andy Rooney

The best gift of all: the presence of a happy
family all wrapped up in one another.

Mutual Moments

Christmas is like a microwave dinner:
  It's here before you're really ready for it.
                                        Robert Orben

An informal survey shows that what most
people want for Christmas is two more weeks
                to prepare for it.
                                        Bob Stanley

Christmas in our house takes two months to
prepare for and one month to recover from.
                                Dorothy Walworth Crowell

Once a year it's Christmas Day.
  Maybe things are best that way.
                                        Kay Riley

The nice thing about a gift of money is that
it's so easily exchangeable.

Arnold Glasow

Santa Claus comes under many names:
Kris Kringle, Saint Nicholas, Mastercard....

Phyllis Diller

It will be a good Christmas. We'll eat too much,
make a mess in the living room, and throw the
warranties into the fire by mistake.

Erma Bombeck

Dogs seem to love Christmas.

Andy Rooney

I have often thought that it happens very well
that Christmas should fall out
in the middle of the winter.

Joseph Addison

Christmas makes the rest of the year
worthwhile.

Charles Schulz

Would that Christmas lasted the whole year
through (as it ought).

Charles Dickens

"God bless us every one," said Tiny Tim.

Charles Dickens

Sources

Sources

Abbey Press 59

Addison, Joseph 151

Aesop 109

Anderson, Hans Christian
    118

Andrews, Julie 51

Aristotle 91

Barnard, Charles N. 116

Barrie, James M. 89

Barrymore, Lionel 38

Barth, Karl 92

Beard, James 72

Beecher, Henry Ward 108,
    113

Berlin, Irving 147

Bettelheim, Bruno 98

Bombeck, Erma 114, 136,
    139, 145, 150

Boone, Pat 41, 100, 136

Boynton, Sandra 136

Bracken, Peg 55

Brooks, Phillips 22, 45, 54,
    57, 129

Bryant, Arthur 22

Buck, Pearl 76, 81

Bujarski, Pamela 38

Bunyon, John 113

Buscaglia, Leo 38, 71

Caldwell, Taylor 63

Cantalamessa, Raniero 60

Carpenter, Charlotte 40

Church, Francis 93

Churchill, Winston 103

Clark, Carol Higgins 106

Clark, Mary Higgins 88

Colette 49

Collyer, Robert 148

Como, Perry 146

Cook, Edmund Vance 106

Cousins, Margaret 33

Cox, Marceline 108

Crawford, Joan 116

Crosby, Bing 42, 77, 78,
    107, 147

Crowell, Dorothy
    Walworth 41, 54, 68,
    149

Currier, Isabel 41, 43

Dacyczyn, Amy 107, 139

Dante 60

Davidson, Margaret 79

Davies, Valentine 36

Democritus of Abdera 52

Dickens, Charles 24, 49,
    71, 151, 152

Diller, Phyllis 150

Downs, Hugh 74

DeLuise, Dom 144

Dunn, David 102

Easterbrook, Gregg 59
    108

Eberle, Nancy 104

Ell, Mrs. Paul M. 41

Ellis, W. T. 86

About the Author

Criswell Freeman, is a Doctor of Clinical Psychology, living in Nashville, Tennessee. He is the author of *When Life Throws You a Curveball, Hit It* and The Wisdom Series, a collection of inspirational quotation books published by WALNUT GROVE PRESS. Dr. Freeman is also host of *Wisdom Made in America*, a nationally syndicated radio program.

About Wisdom Books

Wisdom Books chronicle memorable quotations in an easy-to-read style. Written by Criswell Freeman, this series provides inspiring, thoughtful and humorous messages from entertainers, athletes, scientists, politicians, clerics, writers and renegades. Each title focuses on a particular region or area of special interest.

Combining his passion for quotations with extensive training in psychology, Dr. Freeman revisits timeless themes such as perseverance, courage, love, forgiveness and faith.

"Quotations help us remember the simple yet profound truths that give life perspective and meaning," notes Freeman. "When it comes to life's most important lessons, we can all use gentle reminders."

The Wisdom Series

by Dr. Criswell Freeman

Regional Titles

Wisdom Made in America	ISBN 1-887655-07-7
The Book of Southern Wisdom	ISBN 0-9640955-3-X
The Wisdom of the Midwest	ISBN 1-887655-17-4
The Wisdom of the West	ISBN 1-887655-31-X
The Book of Texas Wisdom	ISBN 0-9640955-8-0
The Book of Florida Wisdom	ISBN 0-9640955-9-9
The Book of California Wisdom	ISBN 1-887655-14-X
The Book of New York Wisdom	ISBN 1-887655-16-6
The Book of New England Wisdom	ISBN 1-887655-15-8

Sports Titles

The Golfer's Book of Wisdom	ISBN 0-9640955-6-4
The Putter Principle	ISBN 1-887655-39-5
The Golfer's Guide to Life	ISBN 1-887655-38-7
The Wisdom of Southern Football	ISBN 0-9640955-7-2
The Book of Stock Car Wisdom	ISBN 1-887655-12-3
The Wisdom of Old-Time Baseball	ISBN 1-887655-08-5
The Book of Football Wisdom	ISBN 1-887655-18-2
The Book of Basketball Wisdom	ISBN 1-887655-32-8
The Fisherman's Guide to Life	ISBN 1-887655-30-1
The Tennis Lover's Guide to Life	ISBN 1-887655-36-0

Special Interest Titles

The Book of Country Music Wisdom	ISBN 0-9640955-1-3
Old-Time Country Wisdom	ISBN 1-887655-26-3
The Wisdom of Old-Time Television	ISBN 1-887655-64-6
The Cowboy's Guide to Life	ISBN 1-887655-41-7
The Wisdom of the Heart	ISBN 1-887655-34-4
The Guide to Better Birthdays	ISBN 1-887655-35-2
The Gardener's Guide to Life	ISBN 1-887655-40-9

Wisdom Books are available through booksellers everywhere. For information about a retailer near you, call 1-800-256-8584.